# The Word On Your Relationship:

*A Bible Study Guide for Couples*

By

Jodi Green

Copyright 2019

Jodi Green

www.jodipgreen.wordpress.com


All scripture quotations are from the New King James version, Thomas Nelson, Inc., 1991

**Special Thanks!**

A special thank you to

Renee' Rhodes and Jay Pettit

for their invaluable comments and edits.

Their insights and suggestions

have added immeasurably

to this study.

# The Word on Your Relationship

### Introduction

God bless you for wanting to study God's Word together. Exploring what God says about relationships will help you build a solid foundation for your life together. Recognizing the importance of keeping Christ at the center of your relationship, not just at the top of a list of priorities, is a great step toward success as a couple. Whether you are dating, engaged, newly married, or married for many years, seeking God's Word on your relationship is the best way to be sure you are on the right path.

An amazing number of great books have been written about relationships; even limiting the search to Bible studies for couples still brings up quite a long list. I have listed some of my favorites at the end of this study for you to consider as you continue to learn and grow together.

This study is different from the others in that it simply presents Bible passages on relationships, with questions for you to discuss as a couple. If any of the passages/questions are confusing, look over the list of resources to see if perhaps one of the books listed might target a specific trouble spot. Through this study, may Jesus be the center point of all of life and all of your lists.

## How to use this study

Always begin with prayer. Ask God to direct your conversation in His way and not your own. Also, remember that the lessons are just suggestions on how to break it all down. Don't rush through a lesson if you need more time on a particular passage. On the other hand, don't limit yourself to just one lesson at a time; if you can do several at a time, go for it.

There is space after each question to write out your answers and thoughts. If you need more space, you might want to get a notebook to list your questions, goals, comments, etc. You should also highlight or note any areas that seem to need additional discussion, or perhaps wise counsel. Consider meeting with a trusted church leader, or an older couple who seem to walk closely with God. Never underestimate the advantage of spending time with a couple who has maintained a Godly marriage through the years.

"Whoever is wise will observe these things..." Psalm 107:43

Our minds should instantly be alert to statements like this verse as we read the Bible...what things should I observe to attain wisdom? Do I want God's wisdom? My own wisdom? The wisdom of the world? What do I really want?

Everyone has goals; even a person claiming not to be goal-oriented might have avoiding goals as a goal! So be honest with yourself and with each other about what you really want. Honesty with yourself, with each other, and with God will be a great foundation on which to build your relationship.

**Lesson 1:**

Read Genesis 1:27-31

The first mention of any subject in the Bible is always worth noting. Here are some questions to consider about this first mention of a human relationship:

What is the description God used for man and woman? (v. 27)


What was his first command to them? (v. 28)


Consider: Was this a universal command to all couples, or unique to the first couple? This is a good time to discuss your views of children and family.


What continued commands are given?

Consider: Do either of you have strong opinions/preferences concerning meals, diet and nutrition, pets in the house, etc. that might need discussion/compromise?

What was God's final description for all He had made? (v. 31)

**Lesson 2:**

Read Genesis 2:7, 15-25

How did God make man? (v. 7)

How did God make woman? (v. 21-22)

What was Adam's problem, and what was the solution? (v. 18)

What words describe what Adam needed? (v. 20)

How did Adam describe Eve? (v. 23)

Consider all the implications of verse 24. Describe how these words affect your own relationship. What does "leave his father and mother and be joined" mean? What does "one flesh" mean?

What is the significance of being naked and not ashamed? (v. 25; dig deeply on this for far-reaching meaning)

**Lesson 3:**

Read Genesis 3:1-13

How was Eve fooled? (v. 1-5)



Was Adam fooled too? (v. 6)


Consider the first woman's influence on her husband and the implications for your own relationship.



Why were they suddenly ashamed in each other's presence? (v. 7; consider the impact of sin on your relationship)


How did Adam handle his first opportunity to confess his sin? (v. 12)

How did Eve handle hers? (v. 13)

Consider: Do you tend to take responsibility when you are wrong? Does your partner readily take responsibility?

*Note: It is not only useful, but urgent in our Christian lives to study all of God's Word. We are skipping over many important truths in order to focus specifically on what God says about relationships. Make a plan to come back and study all of it in context after this study is complete. Old Testament 101 is a good place to start.

**Lesson 4:**

Read Genesis 3:16-24

Read verse 16 in several translations. Write out the one that helps you understand it best. We will compare it later to other passages.

Read verses 17-19 again. Discuss the two-pronged sin of Adam and the implications.

How did Adam and Eve fail each other?

Read verses 20-24 again. Consider how our restored relationship with God and with each other always begins with confession which leads to repentance.

What does it mean to confess?

Did Adam and Eve really confess?


Presumably, being confronted by God would inspire confession, although that was not their initial response. How are we usually confronted in our sins? What is our usual response?

**Lesson 5:**

Part 1: Read Genesis 4:19-24

This is the account of the first instance of bigamy. Though not specifically condemned in this passage, discuss whether it was God's plan. Give reasons for your answer; why do you believe this to be true?

Part 2: Consider Genesis 6-9, the account of the flood. (If you are already very familiar with this passage, you don't necessarily need to reread all of it.) With so many specific stories of Bible couples, why do you think Noah's wife is hardly mentioned? Spend some time discussing a wife's response when her husband is given a great task by God. For example, how would she know if it were truly from God?

Part 3: Read Genesis 12:1-5

Consider Sarai's response, which is also not mentioned in scripture. How should a wife respond? Does the wife's opinion matter in these types of situations?

What if the husband were convinced that a message was from God, but the wife was either not convinced or not certain?

*Further study may bring some clarity to this issue; it comes up several times in scripture and in this study. If you don't feel you have a good understanding on this issue, make a note to come back to it after you've completed the study.

**Lesson 6**

Read Genesis 12:10-20

Here is an example of when both the husband and the wife are wrong.

Consider: Was it wrong for Abram to go to Egypt since God had not instructed him to? Look back to review God's last instruction to Abram.

Why did Abram go to Egypt?

Is it ever right to make decisions of any kind without clear direction from God?

From verses 11-13, how did going down to Egypt affect Abram's integrity?

Is honesty always the best policy?

Discuss the value of complete honesty. What might have been the result of complete honesty in this situation?

What was the first result of Abram's and Sarai's lie? (v. 14-16)

What happened next? (v. 17)


How do you think Pharaoh found out they had lied? (v. 18)


What finally happened? (v. 19-20)


Discuss the implications of God's protection of Sarai even when Abram was wrong.



What were the two parts to Abram's sin?



Did Sarai respond appropriately?



How do the results show God's mercy and His judgment?

**Lesson 7**

Read Genesis 16:1-16

Consider again that there are amazing insights into God's plans for the nations, His character, His dealings with individuals, and much more in a complete "line upon line, precept upon precept" study of His Word (Isaiah 28:10). Our purpose in this study is simply to seek out passages that focus specifically on relationships. Hopefully you will establish a regular Bible study plan together and apply the "precept upon precept" idea set forth in scripture.

In Genesis 16, the husband and wife are both wrong again.

It is appalling for most of us in Western society to consider some of the ancient marital customs like this one. Do we have any modern-day marital customs that might shock ancient believers in the same way?

Where had Sarai acquired Hagar?

Why do you think Sarai was so desperate for children?

How did Abram respond to Sarai's idea?

Discuss again the importance of seeking God's will before making decisions.

Describe the immediate effects of this disastrous decision on each of the 3 participants. (v. 4-6)

Note on the last section, verses 7-16: God provided for Hagar, who presumably had few choices. Do you happen to know how the prophecy of verse 12 still affects the entire world to this day?

**Lesson 8**

Read Genesis 17:1-27

Note their name changes in verses 5 and 15-16 and what they mean. It is also worth discussing at some point your views on circumcision, especially if you have sons.

Another interesting fact: note their ages in verse 17. Look back to find their ages when their story begins.

What was Abraham's first request of God after hearing His promises? (v. 18)



What was God's answer? (v. 19)



Why do you think God continued to bless Abraham and Sarah and show mercy despite their mistakes?



How could these truths encourage you in your own relationship?

**Lesson 9**

Read Genesis 18:1-15

Write any further impressions about Abraham's and Sarah's faith and actions. One reason to examine their relationship and lives is that they are held up as examples in the New Testament. So reflecting upon their life together and their responses to God's plan for them is worthwhile.

**Lesson 10**

Read Genesis 19:1-38

Although this passage does not specifically address relationship issues, there are many lessons about a man who has put his family in a spiritually and morally compromised situation.

Discuss the implications of Lot's decision to raise his family in Sodom.

Discuss why his grown children dismissed his urgent message. (v. 12-14)

From verses 17-20, how and why was Lot still arguing for his own desires?

From verse 26, did Lot have any responsibility for his wife's death?

This story ends in a very sordid and shocking way (v. 30-38). Discuss how Lot's daughters could have grown up believing that this action would be noble for their family. Were their actions right or wrong? Were their motives good or bad? How could they have known the right way spiritually and morally?

**Lesson 11**

Read Genesis 20:1-18

Here is another big miss for Abraham and Sarah.

Interesting note: Genesis 20:12 states their real relationship. Discuss the ramifications of half-truth before God, each other, and society.

Also, how did God protect Sarah and Abraham as well as His plan for their family and the world?

*Something else to consider: Why do you think an 89-year-old woman would be so attractive to so many men? There are many opinions on this.

## Lesson 12

Read Genesis 21:1-21

Try to describe Abraham's and Sarah's relationship to the Lord at this point.

Consider closely verses 9-12. Discuss God's response to Sarah's demand and Abraham's feelings about it.

How did God encourage Abraham? (v. 13)

How did God provide for Hagar and Ishmael? (v. 14-21)

Consider God's provision even in the face of human error. This is a big part of God's grace and mercy continually shown in scripture and in our own lives.

**Lesson 13**

Read Genesis 24

Why did Abraham want Isaac to marry someone from his own family?

Discuss similarities and differences between your two families and how they might affect your relationship. Invest some time and thought in this discussion.

**Lesson 14**

Read Genesis 25:19-21

What was Isaac's prayer for Rebekah?

What are some cultural things a husband might pray for his wife in today's world?

What are some cultural things a wife might pray for her husband today?

Note verses 27-28. More on that later.

**Lesson 15**

Read Genesis 26:1-11

How does the sin of a father affect his children? (Note that Abraham's dishonesty in this exact same situation happened before Isaac was even born.)

Why did Isaac lie about Rebekah?

Do you have any fears that might cause you to lie or sin in some other way?

From verse 12, discuss God's forgiveness and blessing (again!) even when we sin.

Discuss again what Rebekah (and Sarah) may have felt in those situations. How would you feel?

**Lesson 16**

Read Genesis 27

What was the root of this family tragedy and how did it get so out of hand?

How did Isaac's and Rebekah's views on truthfulness affect their relationship and their family?

Discuss honesty in your relationship.

Pray for honesty in your own heart. Are there personal areas where it is even possible to deceive yourself? Do you see any roots of dishonesty in each other?

## Lesson 17

Read Genesis 28:1-9

How did Isaac try to make the situation right?

Whom did Esau marry, and why?

**Lesson 18**

Genesis 29-33

The story of Jacob and his wives is long and complicated, with many potential lessons. Read it section by section and note what comes to mind about your own relationship. Here are some suggestions:

How did Jacob fall for Rachel? (29:1-17)



Remind each other what initially attracted you. List the qualities you noticed in each other. Keep these lists handy for future reference.



What happened to Jacob? (29:18-25)


*How on earth do you think he didn't notice he had the wrong woman until the next morning?!

Also, discuss God's law of sowing and reaping (Galatians 6:7).

What was the agreed upon solution between Jacob and Laban? (29:26-30)


How do you think Leah and Rachel felt about all of it?


This might be a good place to discuss how social customs in relationships can be opposite of God's plan and purpose.


Make sure your own views of relationships and marriage come from God's Word and not from society.

Discuss envy and jealousy in Jacob's family. (29:31-30:24) Do either of you struggle with jealousy? What are some practical solutions? (Hopefully having sex with multiple partners will not occur to either of you as helpful!)


Commit again to come back and study all of God's Word, not just the parts that seem to apply directly to your present situation. So much is missed when we lift out particular topics rather than studying the whole. Old Testament 101 is a good place to begin.

**Lesson 19**

Part 1: Read Exodus 4:24-26

This is the only account of Moses and his wife, Zipporah. If you need to review how Moses, an Israelite, had married a Midianite, this would be a good time to do that (Exodus 2:11-22). A review of how God's people ended up in Egypt as slaves might be helpful as well (Genesis 37-Exodus 1).

For this lesson, consider why Moses would have failed to circumcise his own son. How would Zipporah have known that this failure could be the reason God stopped to punish Moses?

What do you think she meant in verse 26? (If you look up any commentaries on this incident, you will find there are many interpretations of this passage.)

Why do you think God gave us this snapshot of Moses and Zipporah?

This was obviously a conflict in their marriage. Discuss how God's dealing with the failure of one spouse affects the other.

God's language in verse 24 is very strong. Why do you think He tried to kill Moses? Examine your views about God's strength and power. If He had wanted to kill Moses, would it have been difficult for God?

Part 2: Read Exodus 18:1-9

Apparently Moses had not taken his family to Egypt. Give some thought to what may have happened between Moses and Zipporah between Exodus 4:26 and 18:1.

**Lesson 20**

Read Exodus 20:14

Hopefully, during your dating and engagement, the idea of cheating on each other will seem impossible. But consider Matthew 5:27-28, with all of the implications, including pornography. Discuss your feelings on this.

*Note: we are skipping Leviticus and the law books that have some specific commands for marrying and divorcing. So many interesting precepts are found in these, and an exhaustive study can be very beneficial. For our purposes now, however, we will continue with case studies.

**Lesson 21**

Next we will look at the precious book of Ruth. Read Ruth together, taking as long as you need. Then read Kathy Nelson's book, 5 Things. Spend time discussing the concepts; this should take several sessions.

Notes on Ruth (depending on the stage of your relationship, different ideas may seem more relevant than others):

**Lesson 22**

Read 1 Samuel 1:1-18

How does violating God's plan for marriage cause trouble (as we've seen in so many of these stories)?

Does Elkanah seem to understand Hannah's grief and depression? Discuss the tendencies you each have in response to the other's upsetting situations. Is there any room for improvement?

How is Hannah's depression resolved?

Are there occasions in a relationship when a spouse is powerless to help and both the husband and the wife must rely on God?

# Lesson 23

Read 1 Samuel 25:1-44

(For additional insights, see my blogpost on Abigail at www.jodipgreen.wordpress.com)

What if one spouse is right and the other is clearly wrong? How can you resolve the issue?

How could this entire disaster have been avoided?

How did God reward Abigail?

**Lesson 24**

Read 2 Samuel 6:1-23

(The first 15 verses are for context.)

Why did Michal, David's first wife, despise David?



Can there be times when one spouse's acts of devotion to God might cause problems for the other spouse?



How did Michal express her displeasure?



How did David respond?



How did God respond?



Could this situation have been avoided?

**Lesson 25**

Part 1:  Read 2 Samuel 11:1-27

How did David get himself into such a mess?



Did Bathsheba have any culpability? (Consider why she was bathing in plain view.)



How could it have all been avoided?



How did God feel about it?



Part 2:  Read 2 Samuel 12:1-25

How did God confront David with his sin?


What is our usual response when someone reveals or points out sin in our lives?

**Lesson 26**

2 Samuel 13-19

Pick almost any passage in these chapters and note the family chaos caused by ignoring God's plan for marriage (one man and one woman). Even though God did not directly condemn David for polygamy, He certainly allowed the consequences of David's bad judgment in marriage. Again, culturally this was a very widely accepted practice with social and political advantages.

Discuss any other cultural ideas about marriage that are accepted by society but not by God.

Notice that David was called, "a man after God's own heart" by God Himself (1 Sam. 13:14). Discuss how a person might be pleasing to God in spite of their personal mistakes.

How might this concept relate to your relationship?

**Lesson 27**

Read 1 Kings 11:1-13

What turned Solomon's heart away from God?

Discuss the potential influence of a spouse, both for good and for evil.

Note: many couples read Song of Solomon on their honeymoon for its erotic appeal. However, is it realistic to believe that Solomon was able to make each of his one thousand wives/concubines feel special and loved?

**Lesson 28**

Read Job 1-2

Note especially Job's wife's response. Spend some more time discussing how a spouse might encourage or discourage in times of trouble.

**Lesson 29**

Psalms and Proverbs

You likely won't have time to study or even read all 181 chapters of these two important books before your wedding. But since Jesus said the two greatest commandments were

1.) Love the Lord your God, and

2.) Love your neighbor as yourself (Mark 12:30-31),

Psalms and Proverbs provide excellent daily devotions to help you both obey these two commands. So, plan to read/study from these two rich sources throughout your life together. I'm currently finishing a devotional book on Proverbs, with plans to write one on Psalms as well, so, hopefully, later this year I will have those ready.

For today's lesson, start with Psalm 1, and write down some impressions of how these truths might impact your relationship.

**Lesson 30**

Part 1:  Read Proverbs 1

Every verse of Proverbs is about Godly wisdom in every facet of life. It will be very wise to study the entire book together; each chapter will give you many topics to discuss together and grow in God's wisdom. The book of Proverbs conveniently has 31 chapters: one for each day of the month. So it is simple to read/study Proverbs according to the day of the month.

Write down a few commands from chapter one.




Part 2:  Read Proverbs 21:19 and 25:24

What does it mean?




How can it be avoided?

Why do you think there are no specific warnings about a contentious husband? (Keep in mind how many verses there are in Proverbs, basically in every chapter, about recognizing and avoiding fools of either gender.)

Part 3: Read Proverbs 31

How is this chapter applicable to both husband and wife?

**Lesson 31**

Read Proverbs 5:15-23

Discuss again the urgency of faithfulness to each other on every level. Discuss specific ways to keep yourself and each other from temptation. (More on this in 1 Corinthians 7 later in this study)

It is also worth noting that in Proverbs, the warnings are always against a woman seducing a man to sin, not a man seducing a woman. Why do you think that all of the warnings are to men?

**Lesson 32**

Song of Solomon

Enjoy this one if you are already married or after the wedding if you are not! (Try to overlook the 700 wives issue☺!). If your relationship is currently in the dating stage, I recommend waiting on this lesson.

**Lesson 33**

Part 1: Read Hosea 1-2

Also, read Hosea 14:9, the last verse.

Since this is a study of what the Bible says about relationships, we won't leave out this complicated account. It is possible that Hosea had already asked God if he could marry Gomer, and God simply consented. We don't know the answer to that from scripture, though. No matter how you interpret God's plan for Hosea, it is difficult to understand why God would have led him that way.

Why did God want Hosea to marry Gomer?

How does this story illustrate grace and mercy (both God's and each other's)?

As always, skipping over large portions of the Bible in order to isolate a topic is tricky. So, even though we are trying to read and study the passages on relationships, commit again to come back and study the whole. It will give you even greater insights into any topic you might study.

Part 2: One more passage to consider: Malachi 2:13-17. Write out any thoughts that come from these verses.

Note: there are many other passages about relationships that you will come to when you study the entire Bible. I am not including all of them because I really want you to study the rest in context.

**Lesson 34**

Read Matthew 1:18-25

How were both Joseph and Mary sensitive and obedient to the Lord?

Review questions (from Lesson 5):

What are some ways we can know if a message is from the Lord or just our own thoughts?

How could you evaluate a claim by your spouse that he or she received a message from God?

**Lesson 35**

Matthew 5-7

This is another passage to perhaps discuss in sections if that is better for your schedule.

Even though the famous Sermon on the Mount in these chapters is not always directed specifically to relationships, the basic Biblical principles of Godly living are always worth building upon. This passage should be considered more a description of the life "hid with Christ in God" rather than a checklist to try to follow.

Read Matthew 5:23-32

Discuss how understanding this passage affects each of you individually and as a couple. Review any trouble spots that may have come up over this principle.

As you have time, discuss all of these chapters together. Make notes on how these principles affect your relationship with God and with each other.

**Lesson 36**

Read Matthew 19:1-9

What did Jesus say about marriage?




What did He say about divorce?




Did He say that a person should divorce if his or her spouse commits adultery?





*Train your mind to read carefully and thoughtfully, noticing what is actually stated. Keep opinions about a passage separate from the passage itself. In other words, avoid trying to mold God's Word to fit your opinion or the present culture.

**Lesson 37**

Read Mark 10:1-12

Another look at Jesus' teaching on marriage and divorce.

Are there any added principles in Mark's account?

If you come back later and study the entire New Testament (New Testament 101 is a good place to start!), you will see the continuity among the gospel writers. It's definitely worth the time to study more deeply.

**Lesson 38**

Read Mark 11:25-26

Discuss the principle of forgiveness in your relationship with each other and with others. Make sure neither of you has any roots of bitterness toward anyone.

Consider: does a person have to apologize or be sorry in order to be forgiven?

How does it impact your relationship to apologize for offenses?

Discuss the differences in the wording of these apologies:

"I'm sorry; I was wrong."

"I'm sorry you misunderstood me."

"I'm sorry if I hurt you."

**Lesson 39**

Read Luke 1:5-25, 57-66

How did God describe Zachariah and Elizabeth?

What trouble did they have?

What great work did God give to them?

What was their response?

Does it seem they were unified in their task?

Discuss again how your relationship is affected both by troubles and by ministry opportunities.

**Lesson 40**

Read Luke 2:41-52

What was their emergency?


How could a family emergency affect your relationship? Try to think of examples that other couples you know have faced, and discuss ways to handle difficult situations.


How could a different perspective from each spouse be beneficial in an emergency?


Could the differences cause harm?


How could harm be prevented?


What characteristics do you see in each other that could be beneficial or be harmful in an emergency?

**Lesson 41**

Read Luke 6:20-49

Here is a condensed version of the Sermon on the Mount from Matthew 5-7. Consider these principles of the Christian life again.

Are any of these principles difficult for you?

Do you feel comfortable ignoring any of them?

What are some practical ways to apply the most difficult of these?

**Lesson 42**

Read Luke 12:22-34

Do either of you tend toward worry or anxiety?

What worries each of you the most in life?

What encourages each of you when you have anxious thoughts?

How can this type of encouragement strengthen your relationship?

**Lesson 43**

Read Acts 5:1-11

What specifically did Ananias and Saphira do wrong?

Were they in agreement?

How could agreeing to disobey God affect your relationship, both to God and to each other (other than possibly being struck dead on the spot!)?

Can you think of an example in today's world that might be a similar judgment for sin?

Discuss the difference between making mistakes while trying to obey God and deliberately agreeing to sin. Note the contrast in the Bible on those two issues.

**Lesson 44**

Read Acts 18:1-4, Romans 6:3, 1 Corinthians 16:19, 2 Timothy 4:19

Note any interesting details about Priscilla and Aquila, especially their service together and their value to Paul and the early church.

Discuss the importance each of you places on serving in the church together. Will you be attenders only? Do you have any differences in your desire to serve in the church?

**Lesson 45**

Read 1 Corinthians 7:1-16

What priority does Paul give to the sexual relationship in marriage? (v. 1-9)

What specifically does he say about it?

Discuss any mutually agreeable reasons for temporarily abstaining from sex.

Discuss the emphasis on remaining true to marriage vows. (v. 10-16)

Since, hopefully, both of you are believers, discuss the influence you have on each other for godliness, especially in light of the ungodly influences we've seen on married couples in the Bible.

**Lesson 46**

Read 1 Corinthians 10:23-24

Discuss sensitivity to each other's priorities. Do you, as a couple, have agreement in matters of conscience? Since eating meat offered to idols is not really an issue in today's society, what are some examples of social customs that might be controversial for Christians?

**Lesson 47**

Read 1 Corinthians 11:1-16

This is the controversial subject of the husband being the head of the wife. Reread verse 3 carefully. No matter what your personal opinion is at this point, write out exactly what it says about position.

*Note the difference in position and equality from Galatians 3:27-29. The controversy is over position in society and in the home rather than position in Christ, or spiritually.

For a deeper discussion of head coverings, see my blogpost: "Middle School Lesson on Women's Head Coverings."

Write down any other impressions/questions you might have about this topic. We will study it more in Lesson 50.

**Lesson 48**

Read 1 Corinthians 13. This chapter describes the love we are to have for everyone, but should also be considered a suitable guideline for your particular relationship.

From verses 1-3, list a few signs of success in human terms that become worthless without love.

Verses 4-7 describe perfect love, according to God. This list is a useful tool in assessing how far short our human love falls. Write down these characteristics, and refer back when one or both of you needs a reminder.

Verses 8-13 give additional insight into mature love. Write down anything that seems helpful to your present relationship. Note the phrase "we see in a mirror, dimly" from verse 12; write any different translation you may have. Spend some time discussing the significance of that thought.

**Lesson 49**

Read Galatians 6:1-4 and Philippians 2:1-4

How do these passages relate directly to your relationship as well as general Christian living?

**Lesson 50**

Read Ephesians 4:1-3, 32

How would applying the list in verse two affect your relationship?

What are some practical ways to apply keeping the "bond of peace" in your relationship?

**Lesson 51**

Read Ephesians 5:15-33

Again, no matter how you interpret these verses, there is no getting around what they clearly say. It may be a good time for you to discuss what value and credibility each of you gives to obedience to God's Word. Is it true? Is it all true? Do you want to obey it? Do you want to obey all of it? Is any part of it merely suggestion, or does it all constitute God's will for our lives?

Note the first mention of submission in verse 21.

Discuss what it means for each of you. Compare and contrast verses 22 and 25 and the priorities that are expressed. What does this passage suggest for your relationship, and how will you live it out?

**Lesson 52**

Read Colossians 3:12-25

Here it is again. Notice any additions to this passage as compared to the others we have studied. Discuss again how you would apply this concept to the order of your home.

**Lesson 53**

Read 1 Thessalonians 4:1-8

How does this passage emphasize sexual purity in marriage?

How does it relate to pornography?

What are some ways a person might cheat on his or her spouse?

Be sure to make any needed confessions to each other in the area of sexual purity, remembering that forgiveness is the basis in everything.

**Lesson 54**

Read 1 Timothy 2:8-15

Hardly any two people agree on the meaning and application of this passage. Read it in several translations if that would be helpful.

Have you noticed differing applications of this principle based on other faith traditions?

How does your church apply this teaching?

Do you think your church applies the teaching correctly?

**Lesson 55**

Read 1 Timothy 6:6-10

What are your individual views on financial matters? (for example, debt, purchases, luxuries, needs, bills, bill-paying, etc.)

Until the wedding, a couple's finances are usually completely separate. After the wedding, no matter how a couple decides to handle money, everything changes. There are many great books on managing money in the Christian home. I will include some suggestions at the end. Here are a few more ideas to discuss.

What brings financial contentment to each of you?

What are your ultimate financial goals?

How will you decide as a couple how finances will be allocated?

Will you keep separate accounts, one joint account, or a combination? Since we have no specific command on that, agreement has to be reached between the two of you.

How did your parents handle money? Do you admire their financial practices, or do you want a different plan for your household?

Financial difficulty is one of the top reasons given for divorce. Discuss ways you can find common ground on this challenging issue.

One more very important financial issue: the tithe. Read these passages together and discuss your views on tithes and offerings:

Malachi 3:10

Deuteronomy 14:22

2 Corinthians 9:6-11

**Lesson 56**

Read Titus 2:1-8

How do these commands conflict with modern social norms?

Do they conflict with your ideas of women's roles in the home and in society?

Are any of these subject to personal interpretations?

Remember that it is often helpful to read difficult passages in different translations for better understanding. The main caution on that is to be careful not to just look for wording that agrees with what you want it to say.

Discuss your individual concepts of ideal roles in the home. Leave room in your minds and hearts for spiritual growth both for yourself and for each other. Are there situations in life in which compromise is not possible (e.g., whether to have children; where you will live; family relations)? Discuss ways to resolve these issues.

**Lesson 57**

Read Hebrews 11:8-16

What does this passage say about Abraham and Sarah?




How does the Genesis account of Abraham and Sarah emphasize their challenges in maintaining their faith?




How did their faith grow through the years?



How did their faith influence their lives?




What lessons do you see in this passage for your own relationship?

**Lesson 58**

Read Hebrews 13:4

Why do you think this verse is in this list of directions for Godly living?

Compare Matthew 5:27-30. Discuss the many ways a spouse can be unfaithful.

Pray for deep dedication to each other and to God. Pray for each other to stay faithful.

**Lesson 59**

Read Hebrews 13:20-21

This is a good prayer for your relationship. Discuss how this perspective on life could influence your decisions as a couple.

## Lesson 60

Read 1 Peter 3:1-12

Here it is again – the "S" word! Here's another opportunity to look into how seriously you view the Bible, and how willing you are to ignore parts of it. There are certainly issues that were cultural, but again, be careful how eager you are to say, "That was then." Pray over all of it with an open heart to obey.

Does our society still judge a woman on outward appearance? More than men? The same?

Do either of you have strong opinions on the outward appearance of the other (hair styles, fashion choices, healthy weight, etc.)?

Discuss the significance and balance of verse 6.

*Note in verse 7, "weaker vessel", or your translation's equivalent, does not mean "less than". If you look up the original language, it has the connotation in Greek of a more valuable or precious item, like a crystal vase.

Verses 8-12 can be considered more admonitions of how to love each other purely before God. Make a note to come back to these verses during times of controversy.

**What Next?**

God bless you for completing this study. The next steps you take both individually and as a couple can further deepen your relationship with each other and with God.

Go back and review any lesson(s) that may have been difficult to discuss or to understand. Spend some time looking up background passages on issues that may need further clarification. I have included some resources that I hope will be helpful.

Pray. Ask God to bless your relationship. Ask Him to help each of you to prioritize learning and obeying His teachings. He made us; He knows us better than we know ourselves, and He loves us. He is the Creator of relationship, and He is out for our best. Trust Him on that!

Commit to continue Bible study together. As mentioned several times, a "line upon line, precept upon precept" study, as we are instructed in the Word (Isaiah 28:10) is most helpful. I have written Old Testament 101 and New Testament 101 as chronological studies that will guide you through the entire Bible. You will be able to understand God's Word on every conceivable human issue. I hope you will continue to study and learn how to please God in your life together. May many great blessings be upon your relationship as you walk more and more closely with your God.

# Resources

5 Things by Kathy Nelson

What's in the Bible for Couples by Larry & Kathy Miller – has an amazing list of authors and speakers on everything to do with marriage, dating, and engagement; an excellent reference for a variety of topics on engagement and marriage

www.prepare-enrich.com – counseling resources and a blog

www.biblehub.com – for Bible reading and research; lots of commentaries and translations to help with clarity and understanding

www.creativebiblestudy.com

www.freebiblecommentary.org

www.jodipgreen.wordpress.com – not specifically about relationships, but hopefully a helpful resource; includes the Abigail post as well as head coverings for women and parenting thoughts. It also has the free downloads of my other Bible studies.

Old Testament 101 and New Testament 101 (Jodi Green)

The Mystery of Marriage by Mike Mason


*One example of a book I don't recommend is Love and Respect by Emerson Eggerichs. Both the husband and the wife need love and respect, and this book separates the two, presuming that the wife needs more love and the husband needs more respect. I've found that each spouse needs both equally, and the principles in this book do not seem helpful. Be careful what you study!

Made in the USA
Columbia, SC
08 July 2025